SELL ANY WHERE

Live Your Adventure While Crushing Sales

Sell more. Serve more.

DONNIE TUTTLE

Sell Anywhere
Live Your Life Adventure While Selling From Anywhere

Copyright © 2021 by Donnie Tuttle

Published by Book Ripple
www.BookRipple.com

ISBN: 978-1-951797-29-4
Printed in the United States of America

To contact the author, go to:
www.GoSellAnywhere.com

Foreword

"Can I work from anywhere?" I asked.

"You can try," they answered.

Two and a half years later, the sun was setting on the beautiful skyline of San Miguel de Allende, Mexico. I pulled my wife closer on the rooftop terrace of our home and took a breath. Before planning our next quest, we paused to reflect on the previous two and a half years of our life. Our adventure.

In those 30 months, we had traveled with our family of ten all around the United States and even into Mexico. We were able to do exploits that only the rich and retired get to experience.

We learned how to ski, surf, and speak another language. We summited dozens of mountains and sojourned deserts, tropics, and alpines. We watched sunrises and sunsets from both of North America's oceans.

This is at the same time a celebration of our adventure and a map any adventurer can follow.

You can sell and lead from anywhere.

You can have freedom, performance, abundance, and amazing fun.

It was March of 2016 when we left all our possessions behind, some of which we sold, most of it we gave away.

When others caught wind of our plan, they gawked, "This is crazy! Why are you doing this?"

Our only reply was, "Why not?"

This book is for those who have a "why not" when it comes to travel adventure and for those with a "why me" after being stuck in unproductive jobs or surroundings.

Either way, you can do it. I will lay out the lessons I learned and help you to create a road map to crushing it on your path to location independence.

The mindset, motivations, and methods – everything is different when you decide to leave the normal for "anywhere." I bumped my head (or rather, banged it against the wall) more times than I can count in my efforts. I tried everything and interviewed everyone, and all these findings are included in this book.

Let the adventure begin!

Contents

"Dream no small dreams, for they have no power to move the hearts of men." – Johann Wolfgang von Goethe

Introduction

My wife, Chris, and I met, got married, and had all eight of our children in the city of Gainesville, Florida.

We had always wanted to go see things, but we were lucky if we even took the hour and a half drive to the beach more than once a year. There was nothing to indicate that we had any hope of this changing.

Something changed during Christmas of 2015.

Just before Christmas, we put it to a vote. Our children voted unanimously to forgo presents that year and instead elected to pursue something they had only seen in movies ... snow!

We drove to Upper Peninsula, Michigan and had the most beautiful, simple Christmas ever! We also had just listened to Tim Ferris's *4-Hour Work Week*, which had us asking ourselves, "What if we could do this full time?"

We never did get the gift of snow on this trip. We did, however, receive the gift of "what if?"

What if … those two words changed everything.

These words were followed by an answer, vague though it was, "Somehow."

The initial plans we made didn't work out, but they did lead us to the next step. This is important, because as you begin your journey, you must attack each opportunity as if it were the answer, while also being open to other possibilities along the way.

If this sounds like indecisiveness, it is not.

On the 18-hour drive back home, we faced the fact that the job I had at the time would not fuel our journey.

As with most any job, I was required to show up at the office every day. Also, our income could not support this new lifestyle (or so we thought at the time) that we were talking about.

So, I was going to have to do something else. The answer we came up with was that I would start a podcast, and it would make us rich and famous. Then we could travel.

It wasn't the most thought-out plan, but it seemed like it could work (at least to us).

As soon as we got back home, we went to the local Guitar Center and bought a piece of equipment that would act as a digital microphone to be connected with my computer.

The purchase does not seem like a big deal now, but it did back then. With eight children, even buying shoes for the kids made me wince. (Can't we buy these $30 shoes instead of the $50 pair?) Before I could deny myself, I bought the equipment.

Within hours, I called the top 15 people I knew to ask them to interview on my podcast. I'm not sure why, but they agreed!

It wasn't long before I was reaching out to other authors, some of them pretty famous, and they agreed as well! WOW! Success, right?

Well, the fame never came, and neither did money. But something else did – an opportunity!

One of my guests received a call from a person who was trying to sell her their coaching package. It wasn't a good fit, but because I was so fresh in her mind, she decided to connect me with the coach.

Our conversation quickly turned into an interview, and as I felt my heart leaping at the opportunity, one of the first questions that came out of my mouth was, "Can I be location independent?"

There was a long pause before I heard, "Yes ... I suppose it is possible."

All I could think was, "Let the adventure begin!"

The journey that was to follow created some of the most vibrant memories for my family and helped me to shatter records and barriers in sales and income levels.

We started with almost nothing (literally, we were camping in tents during our first few trips).

Along the way, we went through the typical new-position difficulties, such as being stripped of every business advantage I had from my local market and enduring the doldrums that come with not selling a thing as I processed and learned the "sell from anywhere" game.

In the end, when I came out at the end of the tunnel, it was to a life that was more successful and brighter than I had imagined. Selling anywhere was possible!

By the end of this book, you will see "selling anywhere" as a real possibility. And you will have a plan to help you get to where you want to go.

Even though we have since settled back into a home at the beach, the adventure continues. Travel isn't just something we do anymore … it is a core value or part of who we are.

And the selling part, I have learned to say "either/or" a lot less and use the word "AND" a lot more.

I can sell a ton AND travel. So can you.

This book is separated into two parts:

>**The first part** has to do with creating the vision for travel and moving toward it with your family.

>**The second part** is sales training and contains the philosophy and techniques that make selling more simple and fruitful. The prospecting process I call "Love Prospecting," as it connects the processes of the sale to the storyline of the pursuit of love.

Use the content as you wish. If something is not "speaking to you," by all means, skip forward. "Eat the meat, spit out the bones," as they say.

BOOK ONE
Visioneering Your Adventure

THE VISION

I have not only lived this adventure, but I get paid to help top executives do the same. I have made the pursuit of purpose and productivity not only my profession, but the very focus of my life and all my studies.

In all my efforts, I have found that those who make their dreams into a reality normally follow a similar pattern.

That is the path I will take you through. It starts with a "what if."

What if things could be different?

Is it possible?

And then, "Is it possible for me?"

Next comes permission. This is where we must overcome any self-imposed limitations and give ourselves permission to do the thing.

Then (and only then) do we shift our imagination to look at the practical and ask ourselves, "How can I make it so?"

The next step is to go from thinking as if it were possible to acting like it.

This is where you *make* your plan, as best as you can. Then you take action, whether big or small. The dream becomes reality.

As you take action, your actions will be met by some outside source (unforeseen help along the way) and together they create momentum. Momentum is the unpredictable multiplier.

Next come the habits that are congruent with what you now know is possible.

Pretty soon, you find yourself passing milestone after milestone, and before you know it, you are "there."

DEFINING THE DREAM

There will be pain in accomplishing your goal, make no mistake about it. But the clearer your vision is, the greater your endurance through the pain will be as well.

This reminds me of the story of Diana Nyad, the first person to swim from Cuba to Florida unaided. She had attempted several times, and several times, she quit. She was in her sixties by the time she completed this journey. During her final attempt, Diana's coach saw lights and asked, "Diana, do you see that?"

Wearily, Diana affirmed that she indeed saw the light. "Do you know what that is?"

"It's the sunrise, "she answered.

"No! Those are the lights of Key West!"

Seeing those lights enabled her to push aside fatigue and complete 15 more hours of swimming! She became the first person to swim from Cuba to Florida unaided, swimming a total of 111 miles at the age of 63.

We all need vision to see where we are going, so that we can endure the monotony of tiny motions that seem to have no impact, and to overcome the pain and everything that tries to coax us into agreement with, "Just give up."

There are multiple ways for you to begin to process vision. I will offer some best practices. Some of them will work for you, and some won't. Think of this like a buffet. You don't have to eat everything, and if you try something that you don't like, you don't have to go back for more.

"If you can't fly, then run. If you can't run, then walk. If you can't walk, then crawl, but by all means, keep moving!" – Martin Luther King

FIND A PLACE

Dreaming requires a disassociation from current reality. It is best done from a place that brings inspiration to you.

If possible, remove yourself from your living or working space when you are thinking on vision. Those places often have tasks associated with them.

Imagine yourself beginning to see some grand, beautiful future, and suddenly your eyes fall upon the unfolded laundry or the stack of bills that need to be handled. Then the sound of your kids fighting comes through the walls.

Poof! Your imagination was stopped in its tracks. Your immediate responsibilities devour the seeds of your dreams, and like newly hatched sea turtles, your dream dies before it ever had a chance to live.

Having a space to dream is so important because often what is happening in your daily life stands in stark contrast to what is possible. The goal of this process is to have a time and space where you can "turn off gravity" so you can ask yourself not "what is?" but "what can be?"

So, if possible, find a setting that inspires you, not one that gives you feelings of doubt, weariness, depression, or difficult labor.

Sit in your car by the lake, find a secluded place at a park, or even a coffee shop will do. If you can't do this, then find a favorite corner of the house at a time when nothing and no one else will compete for your attention.

Rules for dreaming:

1. Do not yet try to figure out how.
2. Nothing is stupid or impossible.
3. Be playful.

Begin your quest. Isn't it interesting that the very word "question" is a derived from the word, "quest"? Every good quest begins with a question.

Countless individuals before you have found their answers and charted their courses from these questions. Allow yourself to think before you answer.

Take your time.

When you get alone in your place, answer these questions.

"Most of us are shooting for nothing and hitting it every time." – Will Rodgers

BIG QUESTIONS TO ANSWER

I call these The Big 5. These are the first questions you need to ask yourself:

1. Who do I want to be?
2. What do I want to do?
3. What do I want to accomplish/have?
4. In general, what do I want right now?
5. What have I wanted all my life?

Clarify your vision with these clarifying questions:

1. What inspires you?
2. Who inspires you?
3. What could you do to meet them?
4. What could you do that would be inspiring?
5. What adventures do you want to go on (alone, with friends, with family)?
6. What qualities would you most like to exemplify in your life?
7. Who do you think exhibits these traits at their peak?
8. Who do you think is worth following or emulating? Why?

9. What three qualities describe you when you are at your best?
10. What would you like to achieve?
    a. Personally?
    b. In business?
    c. Physically?
11. What would you like your family to look like?
12. Where do you want to live?
13. What would you like to have?
14. What would you like to give?
15. What phrases would you like your life to exemplify?
16. What areas would you like to grow in?
17. What hobbies would you like to try, just for fun?
18. What cause would you like to fight for?
19. What legacy do you want to leave?
20. How do you want your life to be?
21. What would be your ideal work patterns?
22. If you did _____, that would make you feel pretty cool.
23. What is something you are trying to grow in right now?

24. If you could accomplish just one thing this year, what would you want that to be?
25. What places would you like to visit in the world?
26. What do you want to be known for?
27. What are the things you believe in most?
28. What events would you like to go to?
29. What amount of money do you want to have at retirement?
30. What people would you like to meet?
31. What do you want people to think of when they think of you?
32. What people do you want to spend most of your time with?

IF YOU ARE MARRIED

Taking the "anywhere" journey is different with a partner than it would be if you were alone.

If you are married, you probably married an opposite like most people do. That means one person likes to spend, the other likes to save. One person is outgoing, the other likes quiet places. One person is adventurous, the other is a homebody.

Nobody is right or wrong. You are simply different.

According to Christian tradition, when two people become married, they become one. Whether you choose to believe this or not, understand that a three-legged race will be impossible to complete if you are not in sync with your partner.

I would advise you to use this exercise to get in sync. In doing something different, you will need to activate momentum by any means possible. My advice is to walk through the questions listed above with your spouse.

As you answer them, you may find that you want completely different things. You will also find common overlapping desires and inspirations. Focus on the overlap.

To move forward, you must make sure that this is not *your* idea or *your spouse's* idea, but an idea that you both own. You must resist the urge to defend your dreams or make your partner feel bad for disagreeing with you. Keep the energy positive at all costs.

VISION BOARDS

In the Bible, God told Habakkuk to "write the vision" and "make it plain on tablets so that he may run who reads it."

- With unity comes clarity.
- With clarity comes commitment.
- With commitment comes momentum.

If Habakkuk had access to the internet and a printer, God may have told him to do a vision board instead. A vision board is a collage of words and images of what you want. It is the visual answer to the questions you answered a couple pages back.

If you are like me, you may have mocked these "magic picture boards" in the past. I did. One day, after I realized that most of my mentors used them, I decided I would give it a try.

Now I have three amazing vision boards that have turned into "Promises Kept" and "Adventures Had" boards, meaning I have done what was put on them!

Seeing your vision plainly is a key ingredient to helping you take inspired action.

Again, there are many ways to define and clarify your vision, but try this exercise. It might be what gives you the clarity necessary to act.

Here are the steps to making a vision board:

1. Find images and words that match the answers to some of your questions (see the first five questions in "Big Five Questions to Answer")
2. Create a collage and pin it to an ugly or beautiful corkboard or poster board (it does not matter)
3. Share your vision and story. Share it with your spouse and your family. Post it in a visible place.

If you are more of an app person, I recommend Canva. Start a project in 11x17. Google the images that match your inspiration, upload them to Canva, and then paste them to your project and create a beautiful collage.

When your project is complete, you can order a printed poster of your vision board.

Rules:

> Nothing is impossible.
> Do not try to figure out how yet.
> Play.
> Be inspired.

DELETING THE PROGRAM OF "IMPOSSIBLE"

The question for you is, "What can you conceive as possible?"

The first step in achieving anything is to first believe that it is possible.

But sometimes we stop before we start. Why? Simply because we think something is impossible.

Impossible is like a program we all have running in the background to keep us from doing things that are too risky. It will stop you before you ever start.

Here is the easiest way to de-activate this program.

Ask this question:

> Is *anyone* doing it or has anyone *ever* done it?

Prove this program wrong! Then find the people who have done it and surround yourself with their company, their books, and their podcasts.

Do that right now!

"If you don't know where you are going, any road will do." – Ralph Waldo Emerson

REMOVING RESISTANCE FROM EXCUSES

Let's get this one out of the way right now: if you are going to do something new, you will have resistance. In sales, we call that resistance "objections." Let us deal with a few that might be dogging you right now.

I want you to see each objection for what it is – an excuse! It excuses you from your imagination and action. This is lazy!

If you are thinking about everything that you don't have, stop. You don't need a lot of money. You don't need to have a lot of time. You don't need great credit. You don't need to be whatever you think. You just don't.

Let's deal with the top excuse:

"I don't have the money."

I get it! I've had lots and I've had little. When our adventure began, we were on the lower side of the spectrum.

In fact, in 2015 when we made the decision to travel fulltime, I was a sales instructor, making about $75,000 a year. I realize the number is subjective, so if you are thinking, "That's a lot more than I make right now," I would point you back to the fact that we have *eight* children.

The question isn't "can I afford this?" but instead, "how can I take a step toward this," or "which version of this can I afford right now?"

If you find yourself saying you don't have enough money, find someone who has already bootstrapped it. That will help you disprove that objection.

Then begin asking yourself HOW-CAN-I QUESTIONS.

Questions like:

- How can I earn enough money to do this?
- How much will it actually cost?
- How can I get some independence from my current office structure?
- How can I do my work in less time so I can do more adventuring?

- How can I find a job or position that will help me do this?
- Are there other income streams that I have not considered?

Remember, you are in sales, and you write your own paycheck!

When you remove your objections and excuses, you remove resistance to your direction!

I have worked with many clients, helping them shape their lives. I find that the clearer we can become in our goals, the less resistance we have in our motion toward something. That means:

Less resistance = more momentum.

I will show you how to have the momentum of a freight train.

SMALL ACTION

The next step is to take a step, no matter how small, in that direction. Do it before you talk yourself out of it!

In order to move forward, the plan does not need to be perfect, only possible.

Much of this book will deal with how to sell anywhere, but unless you have the faith and belief part of this down, you will always look back and talk yourself out of doing this thing that you very much want to do.

Again, I must imagine that if you are holding this book, it is because this is a desire you have.

"An imperfect plan executed today is better than a perfect plan tomorrow." – Winston Churchill

USE THE POWER OF NORMAL

For whatever reason, human beings are wired to return to the familiar. And whatever we perceive as "not normal" we resist.

That is why new habits are so hard for us to adopt. They do not feel normal.

And not-normal triggers a fight or flight rejection reflex. I believe this is also one of the main reasons why visions do not become reality. They feel foreign, therefore they are resisted.

The goal here is to normalize the vision, make it feel normal. Doing so will make it inevitable.

Let me give you an example of how my wife and I stepped into this. When it came to defining our vision for travel:

1. We started only with, "We want to travel. It would be cool," but we didn't know how. We just knew we would do this.
2. Then we asked, "How could we do that?"
3. We found examples of others who were doing what we wanted. We were always

    listening to podcasts and reading books from fellow adventurers like Chris Guillebeau and Tim Ferriss.

4. We saw people do it with used RVs. We didn't just dream about RVs, we took action to get as close to them as possible as if we were actually going to do it.

5. We were not sure we could afford an RV, but it didn't matter. We went shopping almost every weekend. We went into RVs. We laid down in them. We sat behind the wheel, breathed in the smell. We researched them. We normalized the idea of having an RV.

Note: Whatever it is you want, get as close to your vision as possible. See it. Feel it. Close up. Make it familiar. If you can do this, you are less likely to become your own obstacle. Make it your new normal.

I am a casual observer of swimming, as in every four years at the Olympics. I loved watching every single race that Michael Phelps was a part of in his quest to become the winningest Olympian of all time. One of my favorite races was the gold medal he won by barely out-touching the wall ahead of Milorad Čavić.

The thing is, Phelps had no business winning that race. He was in 7th place at one time, and his goggles had filled with water. He was swimming blind. He had seen this race a thousand times, not only in practices and other competitions, but also in his mind. "Play the tape," his first swimming coach would always tell him. He would have the young Phelps visualize every single part of his upcoming race, playing the tape in his head.

When Phelps was facing what seemed like an evident defeat, he did not panic. He only had to go back to the tape in head.

I had my own Michael Phelps moment. It came in the form of a magic house.

THE MAGIC HOUSE

Along the path toward creating our lifestyle of travel, I came home frustrated and tired one day. This thing wasn't happening fast enough. (We had been fleshing out our vision for a full four months.) We needed to fund this thing, and it just felt like it was going too slow.

My wife had the wits to pull me aside for a quick date. After finishing my DQ Frosty, she asked, "OK, where are we … not now, but in the life we are about to live? Where do you see us?"

I rolled my eyes.

"Are we by the ocean, in a forest, by a lake? Where are we?" she pushed.

I took a deep breath. I was going to play along. "The mountains," I sighed.

"OK, talk to me about what you see and feel," she continued.

"What the heck, honey?" I countered. I was clearly not in the mood.

"Just make it up," she went on. "Tell me. What do you see? What room of the house are you in?"

Another breath. "Fine, I'll play along," I mumbled. "I see huge windows overlooking mountains. I am in the kitchen, after a run. I am pouring orange juice."

"Describe what you see," she pressed, happy that I was responding.

Getting into it, I replied, "I see granite counter tops. I see mist rising from the mountains. We are in the middle of the woods, too. This home is two stories. The floors are wood. It is very peaceful."

"What will you be doing on this day?" she asked.

"I'm going to be speaking somewhere, a bigger city," I added.

"And how will you get there?" she ventured.

"I will be driving a black SUV, like an FBI agent," I stated with a smile.

She pressed, "What's going on in the moment you are seeing?"

"I am drinking a glass of pulpy orange juice," I said, fully engaged now.

We continued on like this for some time. And I could actually see it and feel it.

It would be less than seven months later that we would rent a home in Bethel, Maine, sight unseen.

When we walked into the home in May of 2016, I was seeing exactly as I had imagined! Every morning I would look out at the scene I had envisioned months before, as I poured my glass of orange juice.

It was surreal, and we have since practiced this same exercise many times with the same results.

I cannot tell you why it works, it just does. I believe that we are co-creators, with the Creator, and that our imaginations are more powerful than we could ever imagine.

FUTURE JOURNALING

As a schoolteacher, I learned that there is no one way of learning. We all process things differently. So, I offer to you a different way.

> Try clarifying your vision by journaling with a twist.

Instead of writing about recent events, flash forward and journal the future. Here are the steps:

1. Find your place, and make sure it is somewhere disconnected from the sights and smells of your normal environment.
2. Imagine your ideal future, without limitations or boundaries. Flash forward, like I did in the magic house experience.
3. Simultaneously, tell yourself that you have enough of every resource (time, money, etc.) and that anything is possible.
4. Then write about it ... *as though it has already happened*. Write *FROM* the place you are envisioning. What are the things you are thankful for? Write every detail you can.

The only rule:

> You are not allowed to think about "how."

Bringing the Future Here

Imagine driving across the country for a trip to Disney World with all your children. And every mile of the journey, your children fight and fuss, and your spouse argues. When you finally arrive, ready to have a good time, do you think you are ready to *really* have a good time? Or will your terrible drive make an impact on the destination that was supposed to be enjoyed?

How we get where we are going does matter! And who we are in the process matters, too.

That's why it matters that you not only choose your course of action for growth, but also you choose to change your very identity. You must become that person who would, could, and should rightfully expect to be able to live the life you were dreaming of.

People do not normally exceed the limitations set by their perceived self-identity. The ultimate way to adopt a behavior is to make sure it is attached to your identity.

I once heard a story from a psychologist who was trying to help a family to permanently influence their son to be more respectful of his sleeping baby sister. He described the hierarchy of impact with the following levels:

Level 1: "Please be quiet."

Level 2: "Please be quiet because your sister is sleeping and I don't want her to wake up."

Level 3: "Please be quiet. Your sister is sleeping, and we are considerate people. If you are too loud, it will wake her up from her sleep."

The most lasting behavior change is the final example because it is tied into the identity of the child.

Your new behaviors and habits will last longer if you connect them with your identity.

A lot of what you are doing is proving to yourself that you are who you thought you were. You are proving to yourself that you are you.

The good news is that we can change.

You can have what you want, but in the process, you must become *who* you want to be.

When you look at your vision board or read your journal, ask yourself this question:

> "Who is the type of person who does this?"

Then make it your goal to become that person. Whether that person is nice, successful, smart, funny, a great speaker, fit, or whatever, you can become that person.

Here is how:

> **Step #1**: Look at your vision board. (If you don't have one, then look back at the Vision Board and important answers to the questions previously listed.) Describe the kind of person who would live the way you want to live and have the kinds of things you want to have. Odds are, you assessed them to be at a "higher level" than you are currently at.

Step #2: Follow this prompt and write out: The type of person who lives these adventures and has these things is _____ (fill in the blank with as many things as you can envision about that person). For example:

- smart
- bold
- balanced
- together
- fearless
- loving
- healthy
- wealthy

Step #3: Write out "I am" statements from these words above. For example, "I am smart. I am a balanced person. I have my stuff together. I am fearless. I am the most loving person I know. I am healthy."

Keep writing these statements about yourself, even if you don't currently exemplify those desired qualities.

THE POWER OF I AM

I believe the smallest and yet biggest part of your success plan is your self-talk. This is what you say to yourself about yourself, and it will determine who you are becoming in your journey.

I believe the two most transformative words in the English language, when used together, are:

I am.

We all constantly narrate the events of our lives to ourselves. Usually, because this does not occur in the voice of Patrick Stewart or Morgan Freeman, our narration goes unnoticed and unchecked.

You are where you are, partly because of how you narrated your story up to this point. The amazing news is that you can choose your narrator as well as the theme of your narration.

And when you do this, you get to write the story!

- What do you want to do?
- Do you want to have an adventure?

- Do you want to be at home?
- Do you want to crush sales?

Great! Say it. Own it. Then ask, "What kind of person does that?"

That becomes your "I am" statement.

For example:

- I am adventurous.
- I am a traveler.
- I am location independent.
- I am healthy.

If saying "I am" statements feels disingenuous, soften it a little by saying, "I am becoming …."

Challenge:

> Create several "I am" statements that the traveling, adventurous you would say. Then post those statements in a visible place.

(I would love to see your words on display about yourself. Find me on LinkedIn and send me the pictures. Or you can email them to me at donnie@gosellanywhere.com. If you do, I have a special prize for you.)

If you want to hear me speak briefly about "I am" statements and see some of my own, then scan the following QR code or view it in your phone camera:

https://www.thesalesclassroom.com/sell-anywhere-I-Am

YOUR CHOSEN STATE

Your "I Am" statements reflect your aspirational self. They are powerful. But one thing that often gets overlooked is your chosen state, your "way."

Remember the road trip scenario (from a few pages back) where your family argues and fights all the way to Disney World? Of course, nobody feels very excited upon arrival.

That state of being, how you feel when you get there, is the "way."

When you look at who you are, it should be accompanied with your beliefs about the journey. These should be centered around your relationships with family, time, self, your body, your clients, etc.

Question:

> What is the way you think things should be done?

Write out some of these statements. Find a couple that you own and say how they should be done.

- I believe...
- Family is...
- My time with God...
- I respect myself by...
- Working with clients should look like...
- Working with my coworkers should be...
- I believe that the best time management looks like...
- I think travel can be...
- I think the ideal level of business should be...

Here are a few examples to help:

I believe that I can do this job in less hours than everybody else so I can adventure with my family.

Selling should be serving. That's how I will operate.

My time with God and family are my priorities. I can succeed while keeping these healthy and strong.

"It's not just where you are going, it's who you are becoming in the process." – Unknown

SMALL ACTION, BIG RESULTS

Think about the famous words, "That's one small step for man, one giant leap for mankind."

That small step started with a huge vision and a deadline. The "moonshot" by John F. Kennedy was, "We will go to the moon this decade."

Neil Armstrong's step was small. So was the very first movement toward the vision. This isn't rocket science … oh wait, maybe it is.

To quote another president, Teddy Roosevelt, "Do what you can, where you're at, with what you've got." That is exactly what we did.

When we, as a family, allowed ourselves to believe that we were sojourners, we did whatever it took to back that vision up. We did small things, we started taking weekend trips, and we stayed in tents because we could not afford hotels or home rentals.

Yes, I went on company trips with my family and we stayed in tents!

To put this into perspective, it was the first four trainings at the new company I was working for. The whole family stayed at the nearest campgrounds, and every day I was expected to join a couple hundred of my peers wearing a suit.

This meant that for several weeks of training at different points and different places, you would have found me outside of our tent, steaming my suits so that I could get dressed to go be among the successful.

It is important to say that although we were staying in tents along the way, we never believed we would have to stay in tents forever. We just accepted that as a version of what we were going to be doing.

Why? Because we had 100% belief that we were a traveling family and that we would act like one to the greatest capacity within our means.

Small is where it's at, and this can really have big impact if you are able to code desirable behaviors into your "program." If you want to say you are something, then what you consistently do should be the proof.

HABITS

A habit is the smallest unit of success repeated daily that allows you to say, "I am."

Too many people fail at their goals because the proper behaviors were not repeated correctly.

For most of our lives, we have been given our goals by other people, so most of us have no problem adopting arbitrary numbers and tasks as though they were our own.

But we never fully engage because we are not connecting that with our true, powerful self. True goals should be attached to your *being* and your *behaviors*.

Your habits should point to where you see yourself, where you want to be.

Habits that have a higher adoption rate are those tied to your identity, which is your "I am."

Therefore, choose habits that match the identity of your new, heroic, adventurous you.
Examples of habits tied to identity:

- Because I am adventurous, I...
    - take hikes in my area
    - plan adventures
    - listen to podcasts that challenge my adventurous side

- Because I am a traveler, I...
    - visit a travel agent
    - follow travelers on Instagram
    - plan trips
    - have luggage
    - have an airline credit card

- I am the kind of person who is location independent, so I...
    - rent office space in unique locations
    - am able to organize quickly
    - have definite routines and habits

- I am healthy, so I...
    - do the things healthy people do
    - go to the gym
    - eat lots of vegetables

Use these phrases everywhere you can. Post them. Use them for your computer password. Name your dog after them. Do whatever it takes.

Is it crazy? Maybe, but you have chosen a journey that is not exactly conventional! Take the small step!

As we bridge into the "how," I want to tell you that my wife and I constantly spend time doing the activities that you are reading about. It never gets old.

Your vision and your faith should constantly be refreshed. In fact, for the past five years, my wife and I spend hours every Sunday alone in a beautiful location, asking ourselves the very questions you have read.

Side note on the "beautiful location," wherever that is. I cannot stress how important it is to get away from your normal surroundings. Your home and your office are places of work and responsibilities.

If you attempt to dream in these places, beware! You may be interrupted by real things (we call them children) or thoughts or responsibilities. "I am going to travel to…" quickly becomes, "I'm going to travel to the dryer and fold some laundry."

"You are what you repeatedly do." – Aristotle

CHOOSING YOUR EPIC ADVENTURE

Involve all your stakeholders. Be diplomatic rather than just setting your course without asking, or you can end up in some serious personal difficulties as a result.

This is especially important if you have teens, or if your children are super attached to their friends. Imagine feeling the weight of your kids hating you as you are trying to make new business calls.

You never want anyone to be able to blame you, but rather, see them as people who chose to be with you and who have a say in the decisions being made.

We presented to our children almost like I would have presented to a large potential client. For us, buy-in was important. We knew we would face unforeseen obstacles along the way, but we wanted everyone on board.

To that end, we assembled pictures of the fun places we wanted to visit and the things we wanted to do. Then we made our presentation.

I began it with, "Mommy and I were talking about something and we wanted to share it with you and see what you guys think."

We shared with them our ideas, and then asked for feedback of what they would like to do and where they would like to go.

We quickly looked up images of what they were thinking of, talked it through, and added pictures to our vision board.

Starting this way allowed us to be collaborative along the journey.

BUILDING YOUR WORK-LIFE CAREER

Your career is likely be the main financial fuel for your dream.

If I could transfer one thought to you right now, it would be this:

> Do not immediately adopt the mindset that this must be a difficult journey.

Many of us are still carrying the "eat liver to have dessert" mentality from days of old, and I must tell you, if you think it must be hard, you will likely find a way to make it hard.

Be open to this thing being easy and joyful, and you will be much more likely to have that experience. You're still in control here.

How do you want your work-life to look? That is the question. And how much business do you want to do?

The answers are found by reverse-engineering your goals. It is best if I demonstrate this with an example. Suppose you want to make $120,000 a year while traveling the world.

Goal Income: $120,000

- Your average deal size pays $1,000, so you need to sell 120 of them. Divide that over 12 months and that equals 10 sales per month, or 2.5 per week.

The numbers need to be refined even more.

- If you have a 50% closing ratio, and are going for 2.5 deals per week, then you must present to five people. (2.5 divided by .50)
- If you have a 75% appointment to appointment-kept ratio (25% cancel or reschedule), then you must schedule 6.7 appointments per week (5 appointments divided by .75)
- If 25% of the people you reach set appointments per week, then you must reach 26.8 people. (6.7 divided by .25)
- If 20% of the people you dial pick up, then you must dial 107.2 unique people per week.
- If you work five days a week, then you must dial 21.4 unique people per day.

And now you know how to make $120,000 in a year.

You reverse-engineered your commissions and your ratios to find out what you must do each day to hit your goal.

When you look at the schedule you plan to keep as a traveler, you can easily factor in what must be done in order to support your wandering.

If you want to see me reverse-engineer someone's goals, then scan the following QR code or view it in your phone camera:

https://www.thesalesclassroom.com/sell-anywhere-book-promo-reverse-engineer

MY SYSTEM NO LONGER WORKED

Though I don't know who you are or what you are selling, I can tell you this:

> Whether you are in tele sales or used to selling locally or regionally or nationally or internationally, there is a way to sell anything from anywhere.

If your journey is like mine, then I will tell you that selling from anywhere is *not* the same as it was from your comfy home office location. Six months into my journey, I felt like an early American pioneer with a wild beard, scratched up, half-starved, and maybe a little crazy from fighting off the natives and wild animals.

There were many things that I didn't anticipate. If you take heed, you will avoid some (not all) of the certain calamities that await you in your venture.

When I started, I was successful in my local market. This wasn't my first rodeo. I had sold everything from advertising to real estate and from wireless solutions to copiers – and I was a top producer at most stops along the way.

By January of 2016, I was on the steep incline of success with the first opportunity to go anywhere while selling. I was selling a coaching service. My sales were based on calling local people, often by referral, and creating a workshop where I would come and speak to leaders and salespeople.

It was inspiring, and at the end of the workshop, I would invite others to commit to a decision for my services.

That was pretty much the sales cycle, and selling three to ten of these a month created a rather good income, which I was busy doing – until we departed in our travels.

When we started traveling, the actions that had previously led to me making sales was no longer working. I always thought of myself as smart, but it took me a little while to realize that the game had changed.

For example, I could no longer reach out to referrals and sell them in the same manner I was used to. Nor did I know anyone in the local market who could give me inroads to creating workshops. I had no reputation!

In fact, I didn't even know where anything was.

My progress was painful, but I was able to crack the code and eventually become a top producer again.

You can do the same, I am sure of it. I also believe that talent should not be chained to a location or a zip code!

IT CLICKS

I remember when we moved to our first location (Charlestown, Rhode Island), I couldn't get an appointment. As a matter of fact, it's here that one of our coolest stories happened.

One day I was walking along a beach, sulking about all the appointments that would not set, kicking pebbles on the shore. There were so many pebbles, they changed the way the waves sounded. Instead of its usual "hush" sound, the ocean said, "click-click-click-click," as the waves came in.

As I was walking, I noticed what looked like an antique brick. "Wow! Cool!" I thought.

I bent down to pick it up, amazed at what I'd found. It looked like it must be over 100 years old.

When I flipped it over, I was flabbergasted. I let out an involuntary laugh when I saw a name written on the brick. That name? It was my very own: Tuttle.

How cool is that? I found an antique brick with my own name on it.

Right there, in the middle of our difficult time financially (because of my sagging sales), that old brick gave me just enough faith to hang on.

You might not get any bricks with your last name on it, but I will tell you that similar signs are everywhere if you look for them. Find courage and hope in the little things telling you to keep going. You *can* do it!

It would take me another seven months, but eventually, things did click.

DECIDE YOUR PACE

If you are like the rest of us, you will crawl before you learn to walk. You get to decide the pace of your journey.

Let me remind you that this should be linked to what you think is best, to patterns that feel great to you.

I've seen some people go from one city to the next every other week. For our family of 10, that just wasn't doable.

To some, that sounds like fun, but to us, that sounded like a lot of stress. So we opted to do slow travel. And while some choose to use RVs as their means of travel, we decided we wanted to live in homes. We used vacation home rentals as a resource, and we drove from one home to another in our own vehicles.

In terms of how fast you travel, experience it, feel it … it's all up to you. And from there, be open to deciding what works best for you.

TIME AND SPACE

You show up in a different place. You don't know it, but gravity itself has been ... turned off. Things that were logically tied together are no more. You don't know which way is up or down. You are not even sure which direction you want to go or could go. It's all new.

Do you remember the fundraiser events as a kid where some lucky person got to get into the phone booth full of money swirling around them? They frantically grabbed as much of the wind-blown cash as possible until the buzzer went off. Their adrenaline-filled moment usually ended with them capturing only a few bills of the $10,000 dollars that was right in front of them.

If you are not careful, this could be your new approach to productivity.

I was not anticipating that my time and space would be a challenged. Before I understood my new space-time continuum, I felt like I was always fighting myself. I was always arguing with what I wanted to do and what I thought I needed to do.

Sometimes I didn't know which was which. I wrestled with myself:

- Would I have an adventure or would I be a top producer?
- Would I do it today or would I do it tomorrow?

What I learned was "and" is a better word than "or" when it comes to arguing with yourself.

On top of that, my constantly changing workspace told me nothing about what I was trying to get accomplished. (Wait, workspaces talk to you? Yes!)

Each day, a new home with a new environment or new view or new opportunities would greet me, tempting me to experience its pleasures. With mountains, beaches, colorful streets … who wants to work?

Remember the person frantically grabbing dollars in the phone booth? I became him. My work lacked consistency.

I did not know it at the time, but this would create an unanticipated mental fatigue.

The old office space had its advantages. While there, I never had to ask myself where things were or where I should put them. I didn't have to question "what's next" because I just knew it by the pile of stuff on my desk. Calendars, post-its, and notes littered my area in my old spaces.

I didn't understand that all of these things offered direction, so my mind didn't have to constantly process.

Without these "signs" from an established office, you will expend energy on things that used to be effortless. This can add up!

But you *can* beat the space time continuum and effectively sell anywhere. Let's start with time.

For you, time is about to change. It's crazy, but scientifically speaking, you are going on a journey that is going to slow time.

Novelty slows time.

It's a fact. Novelty also simultaneously stimulates and exhausts your brain.

Your schedule will change, depending on your responsibilities, but your time and space are about to undergo a very big change!

"This ... could ... unravel the very fabric of the spacetime continuum and destroy the entire universe!" – Doc Brown, Back To The Future

RITUALS AND ROUTINES

If you watch sports, then rituals and routines will be no stranger to you. You often see them listening to the same song, over and over, to get into the right mental mood before a big event. And they always follow the same ritual.

Mason Curry, author of *Daily Rituals*, calls rituals a "holy and deliberate activity for its undertaker."

Even if you don't see routines as holy, I can tell you that they will become your new home as your physical location changes.

Performance is programmable and orientation is everything. When you leave the confines of safety of your own home and your old habitation, all the things that restrained your mind will also be gone.

When you are in a new location, you will be tempted to say, "I'm on vacation," and therefore you cut loose and live a life that will be different from your normal, productive work life.

Two of my favorite people on YouTube are Rhett and Link. Look them up. They have a song called "Vacation," where they say, "everything's OK, hey, because I'm on vacation."

- I can eat that fudge. It's OK. I'm on vacation.
- I can do weird things. It's OK. I'm on vacation.
- I don't have to work as hard. It's OK. I'm on vacation.

I can tell you that if you live this way for too long, it is going to crash your journey.

You must buckle down and do things, and more importantly, you must live a life that is sustainable.

Say this to yourself:

"I am *not* a tourist – I am a traveler."

Say it again.

You get to do all the cool stuff all the time, so there is no need to be a glutton, no need to live a wanton life, and no need to neglect responsibilities.

You get the best of all the worlds!

If you can live this way, you will prove to yourself that you can be trusted with this new endowment, this new adventure.

In the eternal words of Peter Parker:

> "With great power comes great responsibility."

THE POWER OF ROUTINES

If you have ever had a small child then you know the power of routines. If you have a toddler, I want you to try this. Tonight at 9:00, tell the toddler to go to bed. Then tell them they should have been in bed an hour ago. See how that one works out for you.

When our children were young, we learned that this just did not work. But if the child knew what was coming next, they would willingly go along with you.

Here's how our evening routine went:

> 6:30 dinner time, then after dinner, bath time, then after a bath, story time, and after story, Bible reading and prayer, then bed.

By this time, the kids were falling fast asleep.

When were we putting the children to sleep? One could argue that it started all the way back at dinner time.

Traveling and going to exciting new places can throw off your sleep schedule, your energy schedule, and general overall schedule.

My recommendation is to find some things that are important to you and stick to them. Treat these routines as special. Make them rituals. (For more on this, I recommend reading Hal Elrod's *The Miracle Morning*.)

Here are two example routines:

Your Morning Routine
From 6:00 to 8:00 a.m.:

> Wake up at six, do your workout, read affirmations, pray, shower, and get ready for the day. Have coffee on the porch with your spouse. Get adventure supplies ready for the upcoming adventure, including after work.

The same thing can happen every single day. And it tells you what's coming next, which is work. But before you jump into work again, you need a pre-work checklist or routine such as:

From 8:00 to 8:30 a.m.:

> Read work affirmations, review plan for the day, get leads ready, prepare a sales story to share on the phone calls for the day, and read one success story or testimonial.

After Work Shutdown Routine

After you've worked all day, you're tired and exhausted. Instead of just running back out to join your family, you need to separate again through a shutdown routine.

I like to end my day earlier than most people. It tells me that I am free.

From 4:00 to 4:30 p.m.:

> Quick email check, create list for tomorrow, turn off computer (all the way off!), put phone away, and go on your adventure!

The stuff that happens in between your morning routine and your shutdown routine should be a reflection of who you are. Remember the "I am" statements earlier? Yeah, I'm talking about that.

If you are saying you are a top producer, then you should plan like a top producer. What would their schedule look like?

If you say you are an adventurer, then your calendar should show me that you plan on being an adventurer.

Schedule in a plan to *be* and *do* what you said you would be and do from your goals and vision board.

Summary of Routines
Morning Routine 6-8 a.m.
- wake up at 6 a.m.
- work out
- read
- affirmations
- shower and get ready
- coffee on porch with wife
- get adventure supplies ready (for after work)

Pre-work routine (8-8:30)
- work affirmations
- plan
- ready leads for the day
- prepare sales stories for the day
- read one success story/testimonial
- affirmations

Shut-down routine 4:00-4:30
- quick email check
- create list for tomorrow
- turn OFF computer
- put phone AWAY

Evening Routine 7-10
- Quick Shower
- Dinner
- Clean Up (I lead)
- Read story to kids
- Read Bible to kids
- Read
- Sleep by 10

SIMPLE TIME MANAGEMENT

A simple way to use your time wisely is to ask yourself:

> "What big three things do I need to do today that will allow me to still say that I am _____ (fill in the blank with strong word that defines you and your goals)?"

Begin the day with this simple checklist. We are talking small steps here, not giant leaps.

Try to do these things first in your day and do not leave until these things are done.

Finish on time. If you can't, then you are putting too much on your list.

SPACE, THE FINAL FRONTIER

Neither Captain Kirk nor Picard were able to take down what you are about to face. They both had the U.S.S. *Enterprise*, but you will have to create, tear down, and recreate your battle station frequently.

I have found this to be true:

> Master your space, master your time.

I did not know it, of course, but when I left my previous office space, I was leaving behind my battle station. There is power in familiarity, and our surroundings instruct our activity!

Think about it!

You will likely be moving into neutral space. Even if you bunkered up in your home, your space was not likely designed to be conducive to your work habits.

Your space instructs your time. It is a visual support of internal drivers that lead you to move in a direction. Don't believe me? Try making out with your spouse in a room full of screaming children.

So then, your job is to construct your battle station with the essentials that help you to not have to constantly rethink what you must do next.

Start with how you want to feel:

- Excited?
- Competent?
- Prepared?

Whatever the feeling you are looking to embody as you work, there are things that go along with that. As a salesperson, your script might be an important reminder of your conversational map and talking points, so put this in a prominent place.

If you keep appointments, then have a physical calendar as a reminder of your plan of what you are doing.

Do you do media? Then make sure you have a camera and microphone set up and your background is clean.

Your vision board should be somewhere in your work environment, so you can always see the reason why you are doing what you are doing.

In each space, try to orient these in the same way, so your brain doesn't burn any calories asking, "Where's that?" or "What's next?"

It is imperative that your home office helps you get in the zone, which in turn will make your productivity and your spirit soar!

The home office can be a little tricky unless you are prepared. When I first started, I was plagued by lagging activity and the byproduct of low results.

You want to enjoy feeling productive, no matter where you go. So, schedule-on and schedule-off.

Schedule the things you will do when you are "on" and the things you will do when you are "off." Don't leave it up to random chance, as that will only bring you chaos. You cannot begin to estimate the toll of chaos on your dreams.

The power of having set work hours tells you that you are going to be doing productive things during that time. And having set adventure time is the constant reminder that you are succeeding at doing what you want to do.

Both are vitally important.

HOME OFFICE EQUIPMENT

Some absolute must haves for your on-the-road home office include:

- a good phone headset

My life was incredibly stressful until I found the exact right match. For me, and I've tried at least two dozen, the absolute best Bluetooth wireless option is made by a company called Blue Parrot. Blue Parrot designs headsets for the trucking industry. They eliminate all background sound so that only your voice is what's heard by the other party.

If you are worried about the sounds of small children or pets dampening your show of professionalism, get this headset. It is still the best money I've ever spent on equipment. They run between $100 and $200. I've used several models and currently have the Blue Parrot X T 450.

- a portable vision board

For your office space, a portable vision board is great. Create your vision board, then take a picture (or an image if you have it created digitally) and order a poster.

It will come in a tube, and you can roll it up and put it away when it's time to move.

If you don't have the ability to put anything on the walls, get a trifold poster board (like you used for your science fair projects) and create a temporary battle station.

- a necessary office cover

If you don't have an office and are working from your bedroom, then I recommend doing what my friend Dean does. At the end of his workday, he simply throws a sheet over his office desk to cover it. And abracadabra, work is no longer on your brain!

Some people who share home spaces or have smaller offices get a nice curtain and create a backdrop. Whatever works, right?

These are some ways that you can make your home office work anywhere you go.

If you are constantly changing locations, you need to consider how you transport your supplies back and forth.

You want quick, easy, and reliable. You also want complete protection for your most valuable equipment.

Remember, without it, your "anywhere" journey comes to an end.

I recommend getting a camera backpack because it allows you to bring all your technology back and forth with its many compartments. They're also usually fairly waterproof in case you get caught in the rain as you walk to the office.

If you want to see me speaking about this (watch and download my must-have equipment checklist), then scan the following QR code or view it in your phone camera:

https://www.thesalesclassroom.com/sell-anywhere-book-promo-home-office

OFFICE SPACE

One of the joys that I discovered in my sell-anywhere journey was the joy of being set up in different office spaces in different places.

On your journeys, you may also seek to level up from the typical coffee shop setting (I do not recommend using a coffee shop as a permanent office space). Coworking spaces are phenomenal for this type of work. The environment is usually clean and edgy and fun, and in these scenarios, they typically offer a shared space for about $100-$200 per month. This space gives you a beautiful room to think and to work.

If you're selling, be aware that many coworking spaces actually have policies regarding noise and phone calls. But many of them also have rooms where you can go and make those calls.

I recommend getting to know the people in your coworking space, because many of them may end up being clients or at the very least referral partners.

If you're going to be using coworking space, make sure you know the rules. Sometimes $100-$200 only gets you two days a week in the office, which might not be sufficient for your needs. Also, of course, be friendly and courteous. These people might become clients. You never know.

My absolute favorite office spaces have been outdoor locations. One of the most memorable was when I would park my car on Lake Coeur d'Alene and watch hundreds of eagles fly and catch fish as I carried out my business. My laptop was open and my dashboard became my battle station. The biggest challenge I had was not saying "Wow!" every 30 seconds.

Most obviously, everything hinges on cell signal. No signal, no connection, and no connection, then no sales.

Do yourself a favor. If you see a location you'd like to make your office for a half a day, try it out before your important calls to make sure that your beautiful outside space has good cell signal. Without that, you're done, my friend.

Pro-tip: Even if your phone shows full signal, go there and actually test it out. Those little bars have deceived me more than once.

Once you have your location with cell service, create a Wi-Fi hotspot. Now your computer will pull from the 4G or 5G signal from your phone. Anything less than 4G is not acceptable!

Some newer vehicles have actual wall plugs put into them. If not, you can buy a plug inverter. You can pick one up on Amazon for about $25.

If you have these things, you literally can be anywhere.

If you are in your vehicle, I recommend using the passenger side seat because that gives you more leg room. If you're going to stand up and do any of your business calls or business activities, I recommend not being in a place where there are children screaming, such as a park.

Again, the Blue Parrot headset will help you immensely in all these things. Do not do coffee shops unless you have a sound blocking technology like the Blue Parrot device. These are horrible experiences for the other party.

If you're thinking about using the beach as your office, that sounds great, but I can tell you from experience that you probably do not want the sand that's going to be in your computer afterward.

Unless you can park your car at the beach, then I would not recommend an ocean office. Your car not only protects you from the sand, it's also the most soundproof contraption that you can find.

...

Now that you are prepared for all the things that come along with selling anywhere, it's time to learn some actual sales techniques.

Let's proceed to Book Two.

BOOK TWO
Love Prospecting
Simplified Sales Methods That Work Anywhere

SALES IS SALES

I can assure you that even though you are on an adventure, you will be interacting with individuals and asking them to do business with you. You will be committing to them, and them to you.

As usual, the higher the ticket item, the more emotion and trust required by an individual to say "yes" to you, thereby increasing the importance of you being a professional and not a schmuck.

You do not need to be the best salesperson in the world for this to work. I was better than average, but not by any means the best, and it worked.

If you are thinking that going remote will be no different than what you have experienced, think again! Others say, "I worked from home before," but surviving and thriving are two different things.

At the very least, I can guarantee that you will have to become a master at adapting and innovating.

BIONIC TECH

No matter what technology you use, sales is still hand-to-hand combat.

I was always a fan of James Bond movies. Like most boys, I loved the part of the movie when Q revealed the secret weapons that 007 would be using on his mission. Just as Q would tell Bond not to play with or abuse his new gadgets, I give you the same warning. It is not the tech that makes the sales pro, but the one who uses tech to accomplish each mission.

Your technology should support your mission, not become your mission, and be used in the proper phase (phases are explained in greater detail on page 106). So now, agent 007, here are some of the gadgets that you will be using:

The Handwritten Letter
A relic of old, most people have stopped writing letters, favoring instead to overwhelm you with emails. You will use handwritten letters. They are particularly useful when trying to establish trust with newer relationships or reinforcing existing relationships.

For extra credit, Mr. Bond, you should seal your letter with a wax seal (found on Amazon for $20).

> *Used in the following phases:* Curiosity, Connection, Consistency, Champion

Text Messages

They will allow you to be seen as a friend, because you are communicating the way a friend would. Beware of behaving too business-like.

Text messages should be deployed when trying to unfreeze a stalling prospect or getting those who ghost you to reappear.

> *Used in the following phases:* The Chase, Connection, Consistency, Champion

Memes

These humorous pictures allow you to evoke laughter and quick responses. Deploy with email and text messages.

> *Used in the following phases:* Curiosity, Connection, Champion

LinkedIn

This social media platform will help you find almost anyone you need. You will connect with prospects here, show your credibility, and message potential clients.

Be sure to use the voice message, video message, and GIF functions of the messenger.

> *Used in the following phases:* Curiosity, Credibility, Connection

BombBomb (or Vidyard)

Record 1-2-minute personalized videos to send to your prospective clients and established relationships as well.

Be careful not to over-produce and over-perfect these. Prospects smell sales and avoid it. Your job is to infiltrate by being a regular, genuine person. Don't worry, you look great in video!

> *Used in the following phases:* Curiosity, Credibility Connection, Consistency, Champion

Zoom

You probably know this by now, but you will be doing most of your face to face presentations on Zoom. Master all of its share features. Remember, your visible expression is limited to the box they see. Be solid. Keep your presentations short.

> *Used in the following phases:* Connection, Commitment, Consistency

Bonus Tool – Podcasts

You can either host a podcast or be a guest on them to show your expertise. If you host a podcast, you can easily attract perfect clients by interviewing them.

After the interview, if you like them, and there seems to be a connection, offer to continue the conversation, and assess their needs. You get the idea.

> *Used in the following phases:* Curiosity, Credibility, Connection

That's enough on the gadgets for now. There are plenty of them, but if you're not careful, you'll spend all of your time chasing bright shiny objects and you will forget your true mission.

Make a special note of the tech and where it should be deployed in your process. The most important part of using any technique or technology is that you still show up as you. People can sense when you are pretending.

Using technology should make you bionic, not robotic. Technology is a better servant than a master.

SALES IS A LOVE STORY

Too much of what we are offered in terms of sales training is what I call heavy lifting. It requires you to access difficult strategies and tactics in the moment of battle.

Therefore, the majority of salespeople burn out within their first year. Most of the rest live in the place of marginal, barely reaching quotas or not reaching them at all. Month after month, they spin through the same cycle until they start blaming the company and eventually get another job somewhere else, only to perpetuate the same cycle at the new job.

I have met people who have been able to live in the margins for almost ten years! Ten years of sucking can take its toll on a human being, which is why I have developed a surefire method to help people to:

1. know what to say to the best prospects at the right time WITHOUT heavy lifting and
2. keep people from sucking by getting them to quick success BEFORE they give up on their self and blame their job.

If I could access a story that is already inside of you, then you would reach proficiency levels at a much faster rate than if I was teaching you something entirely new. When Jason Bourne (see Bourne Film series, of the early 2000s) was able to access programming that had somehow been hidden inside of his psyche, he found himself doing amazing, almost superhuman things.

That's what we want to do, but with sales.

Accessing the Love Story File

The file we are activating is the Love Story file. If you grew up in America, you have been programmed with this file. You know it by heart … boy sees girl, boy is afraid of girl, boy becomes confident somehow and awkwardly begins to pursue girl, she is intrigued by his uniqueness, they meet, boy succeeds in securing a date, they connect and fall in love.

My addition to that is this … have eight children, and live happily ever after.

There, you know what you need to do. This is how to become an uncopiable sales genius! It's already inside of your mind (just like Jason Bourne).

I will break it down for you a little bit here. I call it, "Selling the Seven Cs."

Before we get into this, I want to make sure that we are a match. If not, then you will digest knowledge, but like an organ from an unmatched donor, it will not take.

If you wish to "play the field" and be a sales shark, then love tactics should not be deployed in relationships or in business. The end goal here is that you are doing business with the people who you are a fit for, and they are a fit for you.

- You genuinely believe that selling is something you do *for* someone and *with* someone and not *to* someone.
- You must want yourself AND your clients to win.
- You love them and they love you.

If that is you, then you will see yourself in these practices. Embrace them and make them a part of your repeated practice.

Your goal with a client should be a long-term relationship and lots of referrals. If that is you, then here are the 7 Cs:

1. Conviction
2. Curiosity & Credibility
3. Chase
4. Connection
5. Commitment
6. Consistency
7. Champions

SELLING C#1: CONVICTION

In 2002, I left teaching and began my career in sales. My first job was to sell a product that did not exist anywhere except in my boss's brain. I was selling advertising to local businesses door to door.

The plan was that the boss was *going to* get a billboard which *would* drive people to a website. Advertisers on the website *would be* noticed and somehow get business from this.

After the third month of selling, I had only sold a few ads and I wasn't feeling successful. I was also selling a product that I could not see, which further eroded my already emaciated conviction.

I was a flat tire. I had zero belief in anything. When I showed up at a prospect's office, I felt like I needed them way more than they needed me. I had commission breath!

Because of my low esteem in myself and my product, I couldn't get any movement. Just before I quit, my boss helped me get a job selling wireless phones B2B, which began my true career in sales.

Confidence is sexy, and the first sale must always be to yourself. Without conviction in the profession of sales, you are a goner.

Zig Ziglar says that selling is simply conveying belief. So, your first step in sales is to become an attractive suitor and *grow your belief*. You must believe in yourself and your product, and the people you are selling to.

One thing that has helped me (and countless clients of mine) is self-talk. You must believe that you are desirable, good, and noble.

You can reprogram what is going on between your ears. Scan the code below to hear me firing myself up with powerful self-talk just before making sales calls on my Sell Anywhere journey back in 2016. (It's live footage from my least favorite office.)

Scan the following QR code or view it in your phone camera:

https://www.thesalesclassroom.com/sell-anywhere-book-promo-Self-Talk

You must feel like the good guy. You may laugh, but for the first several years of my career, I would call or walk into a new business, almost apologizing for even being present.

This is not heroic. I treated myself as though I was a disturbance, an annoyance, and the problem … instead of the solution!

Trust me, you can't win this way! To exchange this self-defeated identity for that of a rescuer, I often have clients picture themselves as a doctor in a foreign land where the inhabitants are all infected with a disease that will kill them unless they receive the cure. And *you* have the cure! They need *you*!

Now, how determined are you to make connections? You and your product are the cure to a problem that people often don't even know exists. Persist for them, not for you. They deserve you. Show up!

You must also have conviction in what you sell. If you are not totally sold on your product, there are three things that I recommend:

1. Do you believe you are doing a good thing? Are you helping fix a problem that others have? Do you believe in what you are selling? If not, do yourself and the world a favor and find something else to sell. Do it now! Many of us have an internal belief, but to sell like a boss, you must have a belief in your product or service that is infectious.

2. If you are not quite there, I recommend becoming a testimonial superman!

Nourish your infectious sales brain daily by receiving and reading client testimonials. These are real testimonials from people whose stories will supercharge your belief. Read these daily. Memorize them. These success stories are the most important part of your scripting, both to you and your prospect! (If you need to gather success stories from your clients, then send me an email at donnie@gosellanywhere.com with the subject line "testimonial superman" and I will reply with several.)

3. You must believe that you are selling to the right people. I want to remind you that everything in love is optional, even the one you give it to. It is the same in sales. Why sell to people who aren't the best fit for you or your product or service? "Because I need money" is a common response, but that is not a good answer. Yes, you get a commission check, but at what cost to you? You are wasting too much energy over-serving them and giving them too much time, time and

energy that could be focused on the ones you love.

Once you decide to focus on the ones you love, you will notice:

> A) a thinned-out pipeline (don't be alarmed, we can fix that) and

> B) more pep in our step, more ideas at work, and more fire and passion for life when you walk through your front door at the end of the day!

This takes a little figuring out, but here is how you do it. Begin by looking back over all the clients you ever sold and served. Who were your most enjoyable and most profitable? Who were your favorites?

Look for commonalities and create an ideal client profile. When you have your list, here are some questions to ask yourself about them:

1. What industry were they in?
2. What problems did they have?

3. What position did they hold? (CEO, IT Director, Real Estate Agent, Etc.)
4. What were their motivations?
5. What was their personality type?
6. How did they treat you?
7. What were their life values?
8. What was their family status?
9. What did you respect the most about them?
10. What associations do they belong to?

Assemble all these facts into one identity. This is now your holy grail, your pursuit, your ideal "perfect 10" client.

All your efforts and energies will be pointed in the direction of *this* person.

You will make lists of people who seem like this, you will make marketing materials and craft messages that would be interesting to them, and you will find ways to be introduced to them.

Know your ideal clients. Know their language and problems. Know that you can meet their needs. And serve them like their life depends on it!

Create a list of people you should meet. People who need the cure and proceed to the next step.

"Learning to love yourself is the greatest love of all." – Whitney Houston

SELLING C#2: CURIOSITY & CREDIBILITY

Imagine you are single again, or if you are unmarried, and you see your "perfect 10" individual sitting alone at a café … now what? Are you going to walk right up to them and ask for their hand in marriage?

Of course not! Going straight for the kill is not recommended, for a lot of reasons.

Instead of this full-throttle approach, you need to operate with a bit more finesse and respect for others. You need their involvement.

After all, selling, like love, is not something you will be doing *to* someone, rather it is something you will be doing *for* someone and *with* someone.

So how do you get them to meet and engage with you? It's best to deploy curiosity and credibility. In the world of dating, this means:

- you are interested
- you are interesting
- you are not an ax murderer

In selling, there is not a lot more to it.

1. You must first show yourself interesting, and that means being different, better, and able to get attention in a way that is remarkable.

2. Next, show that you are interested. Your attention and your approach will prove that you are not aloof or indifferent. You don't need this person to like you, but you are interested in them.

3. Finally, you must show yourself to be credible. Someone who belongs in their world and is not a threat. Your goal is to get them to say, "This guy is different. I like the way he thinks."

Imagine that someone really wants to meet you and decides to send you an email, send you a canned LinkedIn message, or maybe connect with a cold and awkward phone call.

You probably get so many of these that you cannot count them nor differentiate one from another.

Now imagine someone instead sends you a gift card to your favorite coffee shop or a funny gift along with a note asking for a meeting.

Which person are you more likely to meet with?

If you have been in love and pursued another person, then the answer is truly clear. The first person treated you like everyone else, while the second person thought about you as a unique individual. They took their time. And if they took their time early on, you subconsciously feel that they might be a better long-term partner as they are more likely to take their time with you later.

Those who are good at creating curiosity are what I would call "business romantics." They are different, and different sparks curiosity. And just like the proverbial cat, people cannot resist curiosity.

Creating Curiosity in VIP Prospects

Stu Heinicke, the author of *How to Get a Meeting with Anyone*, details how to get high-profiled people to take time with you. In his book, he states that the ultimate goal is having someone receive something from you in a way that makes them see you in a positive light. You want them to laugh. You want them to say to themselves, "I like the way this guy thinks."

I stumbled upon this magnificent tool quite by accident, from a place of frustration. In our travels, we went through the great state of Maine. We love Maine for all its wild beauty, waterfalls, animals, and adventures. But in business, it was truly an unconquerable land until I decided that enough was enough.

In the beginning of our stay in Maine, I shot out a barrage of phone calls and LinkedIn messages. All the messages were greeted by friendly enough people, but none of them were willing to meet with me.

I finally came to my breaking point after four weeks of effort with no results. I found that people in Maine only trust "Mainers." A Mainer is not someone who has been in the state for 10 years or even 20 years, but a "Mainer" is someone who was born in the state of Maine! And that was not me. If you wanted locals to trust you for potential business, but were not a "Mainer," then no dice.

I went to the local hobby store looking for ideas and I settled upon purchasing bottles that looked like the kind of bottles someone would throw off a deserted island as a means of last-ditch communication. I was going to send a note in a bottle to my prospects. That seemed to fit my situation perfectly!

I came back to my home office and crafted a note. The note read something like this:

> Hi Bob! We haven't met yet, but I was hoping we could change that. I am a consultant who has intentionally stranded himself here for a short time as I help a few local businesses grow their sales teams. During that time, I am on a personal mission to connect with the coolest movers and shakers in town, like yourself. As the new guy, I would love to buy you a cup of coffee. I can bring it by to your office. No need to reply by bottle as I will be reaching out to you soon. I hope you are open minded to meeting me.
> – Donnie

The results were astounding:

> 9 out of 10 people who received the message in a bottle met with me.

Previously, I had a 100% rate of being ignored. Clearly, having a plan to create curiosity in others is a surefire way to pull yourself from the trash heap of obscurity!

There are so many ideas that you could deploy. I do recommend listening to the podcast episode from Sell Anywhere podcast with Stu Heinecke, referenced below. Give it a good listen, but don't outsource your greatest resource ... your own creativity.

To spark this, you can just simply walk through the craft store, looking for something that could symbolize the reason for your desired connection. Have fun! Curiosity is going to set you apart from all of the other would-be suitors, the people who are takers of time and attention. Instead, you build intrigue and start the relationship out as a giver.

Scan the following QR code or view it in your phone camera:

https://www.thesalesclassroom.com/sell-anywhere-book-promo-curiosity

Establish Credibility

To be a possible match for someone's needs, you must be seen as different, but not too different. Things that are too novel are also perceived as too risky. That beautiful person isn't going to go on a date with you unless you seem different but also safe.

You must be careful to mix in healthy doses of credibility into your approach along the way. Before someone decides to meet with you, they must be at ease, feeling that you are "one of them."

It seems like social media was built for this. True, there are a thousand pretenders for every real deal, but that doesn't matter. LinkedIn, Instagram, and Facebook are not your primary relationship building tools. Think of them as your living I.D.

As you approach others who might be unfamiliar, they will most likely decide to look you up online before giving you time of day. When they do, they will decide whether you are a friend or a threat. (If you are invisible, then you are most likely perceived as a threat.)

If you know something about something, put it out there for everyone to see! Social media is a great place to show your credibility. Sharing relevant content shows that you deserve a seat at the table.

Go as deep as possible without losing sight of your goal. Too many people get lost here. They go all in and start to see social media as an "end" rather than what it is ... the "means."

Social media is just a vehicle. So, own as much of it as you can without allowing it to own you.

I will lay out a simple progression of what your plan should be. I will start at the kiddie section of the pool and progress to the deep end. The deeper you go, the more likely it is that you might get caught in the over-indulgence trap, so be careful!

1. **Share good content.** This is easy. Follow cool people who post cool stuff. Then just share it. That's it. They did all the hard work, and you get to reap the rewards. Because you shared something cool, others think you are cool as well. Your goal should be to find one valuable piece of information a day for your ideal client and share it. It only takes a few searches, which can be done in 5-10 minutes a day.

2. **Like and comment.** This is called "social" media for a reason. If you find people

who shared something you love, or disagree with, then let your voice be heard. I recommend using LinkedIn Navigator or Facebook Groups to watch for "people of interest." When they post something, then share your genuine thoughts. Don't just say, "Good stuff!" Leave a comment that actually adds value. Just go from your lists of people of interest or you will get sucked into the social media black hole. I recommend spending no more than 5-10 minutes a day doing this. Literally, set a timer. When your timer goes off, then stop and move on to something else.

3. **Post content.** The rule is to do whatever allows you to share original thought that benefits your target clients the easiest. You have great thoughts, so share them. Do you have success stories about your clients? Share those. Be cautious to share about your client's success, not your own. If you are a writer, then write. If you are graphically inclined, create inspirational quotes on an app like Canva. If you are a talker, then do a

video. This will take about 30 minutes a week. You must make sure not to let the time monster eat you because you were trying to make something perfect. You also must avoid the temptation to constantly look at audience interaction. I have been the guy who posts a video and then refreshes every 10 minutes to see how many more downloads it has had. This is a tremendous waste of time and energy.

4. **Message people.** You can and should use messaging in social media. Just don't be spammy. Follow the way of connection described below, and you should be good to go.

5. **Become an influencer.** Run a group and bring others together. You can gain business from this, a lot of business. It takes a lot of energy, so I don't recommend this to everyone. But if you are connector of connectors, then go for it!

Your Voice of Credibility

Credibility has a sound. There is a voice that, if used, conveys confidence and authority. It sounds like a doctor. Your "doctor voice" is used when you slow your speaking cadence, deepen your voice, raise your volume, and inflect down at the end of your sentence.

Imagine your doctor saying, "We need you to come in for a follow up appointment next Tuesday."

If this is hard to imagine, here is the opposite. Read this in your nicest, most considerate voice:

> "Would you like some more crumpets and tea?"

Odds are, you inflected *up* at the end of the question. The up inflection displays a need for clarity. This is appropriate for a question.

If you do the opposite, then it conveys authority. You have no questions because you are sure of what you are saying.

Using your doctor voice in proper doses will convey knowledge, confidence, and leadership. Try it when speaking about your topics of expertise.

SELLING C#3: CHASE

Really, I would prefer to use the word "pursue" here, but alas, the 7 Cs required a sacrifice.

Most salespeople maneuver prospects into a sales conversation. They trap them, but if someone feels trapped when you are speaking to them, you are triggering the wrong response (can someone say fight or flight?).

How you show up here is where you separate yourself from all the other losers who give empty promises.

Sometimes you must show up as professionally persistent, or in other words, you must chase. Even though you have created curiosity and credibility, that doesn't mean you won't meet with resistance.

If someone is worth your attention, then they are worth showing up for consistently. Imagine yourself trying to get a date with your "perfect 10" again. There are a variety of reasons why your first grand attempt might be met with resistance, including:

- busyness
- poor treatment in the past
- an abundance of good options

In these cases, you will have to prove yourself.

But how do you know it's worth it to follow up? And how do you stay out of "Follow-Up Purgatory"?

> **Follow-Up Purgatory** is the loop of continuous outreach to someone who will never pay attention to you, ever, no matter what.

Outside of no effort, the number one reason for failure in sales is wrong effort. Following up with the wrong people continually is the definition of wrong effort.

If you don't try, then you won't win, right? This is true. If you give up too soon, then you won't win either, right? This is partly true. (Cue up Jim Carrey from *Dumb and Dumber* ... "So, you're saying there's a chance!")

This is where a plan comes into play. To avoid

the follow-up cycle of forever, set parameters. The amount of chase you are willing to give should be proportionate to the amount of value the prospect offers to you.

I recommend a simple touch plan. You should weigh the effort you give directly to the potential payoff. You can't treat everyone the same, because they are not. Create a scale of impact, a rule that governs the amount and frequency of your contact efforts.

The chase could last for two phone calls or it could last for two years. If you are pursuing a career-changing client, then it's justifiable to chase them for years.

But the white whales are not everywhere. If you are not sure of the quality of the lead, give them three attempts and then remove them from your list.

By creating a scale, you will avoid being trapped in Follow-Up Purgatory. Here is an example:

1. **Ideal Client:** follow up forever until you get a "No"

2. **Great Lead:** 8 attempts, then stop or put into drip campaign

3. **Good Lead:** 4-5 attempts, then stop or put into drip campaign

4. **Unknown Lead Quality:** 3 attempts, then stop or put into drip campaign

You should plan out where these attempts might occur, as well as what you will say in the process. Having a plan will lower your resistance and help you avoid procrastination.

This can be put into any CRM, and even if you don't have anything complicated, you can simply use an old-school spreadsheet. One of my clients created a brilliant checklist that included all eight touches.

(It fits a full 8.5x11 page, so it won't fit here. Send an email to me titled: FOLLOW UP SHEET at donnie@gosellanywhere.com and I'll send it to you as a PDF.)

Name	Touch 1	Touch 2	Touch 3	Touch 4	Touch 5	Touch 6	Touch 7	Touch 8	Touch 9
	Call/Msg	Letter or Book	email	FB Message	Call	Personal Visit or Drop Off	Phone Call	Email	Final Call/VM/EMail/Text

The type of business you are in also comes into play when determining the frequency. I personally may try three times in a week. I have several people I work with in the insurance world who will try up to seven times in one single day, and their connection rates are amazing!

What you do not want to do is call someone once a quarter or every few weeks and expect them to remember you. If you are new to them and they are new to you, then I recommend at least three touches in the first week, at least two touches the following week, followed by a final touch on week three.

Remember:

> Each time you reach someone, the numbers reset.

Suppose you have a decent lead and you determined that you would give eight attempts to reach them. If you reached them on the 4th attempt, then you now give them eight more attempts before you flush them from your system.

In most cases, if you get ghosted for three weeks, just move on.

The final thing I will say about the chase is that you need to have something else to say other than "I'm following up" or "I'm touching base with you."

If you need help with this or anything else with "chasing," I recommend you register for my free course on Epic Follow Up. Scan the following QR code or view it in your phone camera:

You have shown yourself worthy of a brief conversation. You have been given an audience, however brief, so now it's showtime!

SELLING C#4: CONNECTION

As with a dating scenario, you may know what a "perfect 10" looks like, acts like, and sounds like, but until you get close enough to actually talk to them, you don't really know if they are a fit. The same holds true with any business relationship.

Let's remember where we are in the relationship.

- You have shown that you are interesting and interested.
- You have given enough credibility to have a brief conversation with a new potential relationship.
- You are ready for a brief conversation, not a marriage proposal. Remember, you don't know them, and they don't know you. You don't know for sure that you can fix their problems, let alone if they have any.

With your connection, if you move too slow you seem aloof, but move too fast and you come off as desperate. Neither of these things win in love or sales. Too many people get nervous and act unnatural when they finally get their first connection and their deal dies on impact. But that is not you!

Before we get into the particulars, I want to remind you of the right mindset, and it is this:

> You belong here. They want to talk to you. It's possible that they need you. You love serving people like the person you are about to talk to. You are just looking for a few open-minded individuals. You only work with the cool ones.

Now that I reminded you of this, you need to remind yourself. Literally say these phrases out loud to yourself before you make your connection attempts.

I keep phrases like this written down on a flashcard next to my workspace, and I have my clients do the same. I have said these phrases thousands of times, and it really, really helps.

There is no one-size-fits-all when it comes to connection, so I will be general. Sometimes, the connection is broken into multiple meetings or condensed into one or two meetings. We will use the main structure that fits almost any sale.

The first connection should be used to gain an actual appointment. That first appointment (connection #2) is a "factfinder" appointment to gain understanding with questions. The next connection objective is to present your solution and ask for their business.

Each stage should be a conversation designed to avoid fluff and move them toward the next stage. The end goal is commitment to a solution.

Connection #1: The First Interaction

The goal of Connection #1 is to set the appointment.

Have you ever tried something new and been in a situation of not knowing what's next? Imagine paying for a burro ride down the rim of the Grand Canyon and the person simply took your money and gave you a donkey. Without any instructions, that would be pretty scary, right?

We must accept our role as expert guides in the sales process. This means constantly letting prospects know what is next. Each connection should be a balance of intrigue/interest and a predictable, narrated path.

So, what should you say? Good question! What would you say if you were meeting someone you were attracted to? You don't need any scripts (even though I will give you examples), you just need to know what you would say in a real love pursuit.

Let's take that phrase and put dress shoes on it, and there you go!

> "Hi, I think you look really pretty. Would you be willing to go out on a date sometime so we can chat?"

Business version:

> "I noticed your ad and thought, 'Wow, I like how this guy serves our community!' I serve people like that all the time at my company, and I thought, I need to get to know this guy. Would you be open to grabbing a coffee one morning this week? My treat!"

It really is that simple! How you approach this scenario in real life is how you should approach it in sales!

Why do people avoid salespeople? Because we make things weird! We make things weird when we try to grow a relationship in the most unnatural way.

Just be natural, and you will find that it goes much, much better!

Here is how I would structure my first connection:

If you want an easy structure, here you go. I called it "Why-Why-What Next."

1. Why I called...
2. Why you should care....
3. What's next is...
4. What makes sense to you?

Remember, your primary goal is to get the meeting. Don't talk too long and do not sell.

Here are some examples of how you might touch it up for a few different groups.

Champion

Let's start with the easiest and most effective way to connect, through champions! (To see how to set this up, skip forward to the 7th and final "C.")

I will discuss techniques in the Selling C#7: Champions section for how to obtain this, but your champion is basically rolling out the red carpet, copying you and your prospect on a text message or email saying, "You two should meet!"

This would be like a blind date set up. You are just acting as a willing and open-minded participant to a connection that your champion said should happen.

Without a script, what would you say in a blind-date scenario? Probably you or your date would begin conversation with questions like:

1. So how do you know Donnie? (That's interesting!)
2. What do you do? (That is cool!)
3. How long have you done that? (Awesome!)
4. What are your challenges?
5. What do you believe?

It's pretty much the same as should happen in your prospecting scenario! There are no lines to remember (although I will help you with some scripting samples).

Here are business-related questions to ask your new connection:

1. So how do you know Donnie? (That's interesting! I know him through_____)
2. What do you do? (That is cool! I help that type of person with _____)
3. How long have you done that for? (Awesome!)
4. What are your challenges? (That is exactly what I help people with. We should talk!)
5. I believe _____. Does that align with what you believe?
6. Let's set up a time to do a deep dive to see if we should work together. Would you be open to that?

First Connection – Warm Lead

A warm lead is anyone you have sparked curiosity in. This could have happened through a LinkedIn message, a video message, a handwritten letter, or a gift of any variety.

You have less than one week to strike after your initial display of shock and awe. The script is pretty much the same as above, but instead of building trust through the common relationship of Donnie (the referrer), you are connecting with the emotion that you evoked through your initial contact.

1. Did you receive the (letter, sword, video, boombox, etc.)?
2. What did you think?

Then start using the easy but effective "Why-Why-What Next" script.

- Why I called...
- Why you should care....
- What's next is...
- What makes sense to you?

It might sound like this:

> "Bob? Hi Bob! This is Donnie. Donnie Tuttle? (inflected like a question on purpose.) Did you receive what I sent to you? What did you think? Great, the reason I called is that I am connecting

with a few IT managers in the area about what they are doing for their document services. I help IT managers lower costs and simplify tracking and accounting. I don't know if you are familiar with John Smith at Company A, or Susie Smart at Company B, but I helped them simplify operations, and in Bob's case, we saved him 30% in the process! If it makes sense to connect deeper, I wanted to see if we could schedule a call so we can take a true look. Would it make sense for us to have a quick call on Monday or Thursday?"

First Connection – Tier-2 Lead

A Tier-2 lead is someone you pulled from a list who appears to be identical to your ideal client.

My favorite place to find these people is from trade associations, for trade associations are industry peers who gather together to run their businesses more efficiently. These are what some would call "target-rich environments."

If I were looking for IT managers, I might research trade associations for IT professionals.

Then, find member lists or exhibitor lists and begin the process.

Here is how a first connection via LinkedIn might look:

> Msg 1: Hi, _____. It looks like we both serve the same people and have common beliefs. Let's connect!

Wait a few days before sending the next one:

> Msg 2: Hey _____, I'm sure my time is totally off, but would you be open minded about getting together about _____ (the main benefit you provide). Just curious. Let me know.

There are too many scenarios to chase down here. The main thing is to stay on goal. Your goal is to create enough of a moment between you and your prospect to ask for a deep-dive appointment.

Connection 2 & 3 – OWN Pain SPA

Where are you? You are looking at someone and they are looking at you, that's where you're at.

This part of the sale is about calibration. In a relationship, you would never ask anyone to marry you before you have collaborated with them in real life, which may involve many dates, lots of questions, and getting to know one another.

Really, the question is, "Are we a match for each other?"

That's the only thing you need to know at this part of the sales process, that you are simultaneously trying to figure this out while the prospect is doing the same. It's up to you to lead the conversation. But as they say in the old jazz song, it takes two to tango.

If this were a relationship, then all of the dates leading up to the big question are rolled into one meeting.

Although I am trying to lay out a system that does not require you to remember scripts and tactical combat moves for selling, I feel it is important to give this some structure.

Why? Because we have been programmed with so many self-centered tactics that view selling almost like a wrestling match.

Let's look briefly at the psychology and practice of the presentation. With anything, I believe it is best to start with what you hope to achieve.

With the first connection, the goal is to get an appointment, nothing else.

During the presentation, you have a few goals:

- **First goal:** Let them know that they are safe and that you will not try to push anything on them. Rather, you want to come alongside them to understand their journey.
- **Second goal:** Gain a true assessment of their scenario to see if your solution is indeed a helpful cure to their pain. We do this through questions and by being genuinely curious.
- **Third goal:** If you have a solution, then the third goal is to share the solution (this is the shortest part of the process).

- **Fourth goal:** Gain a commitment that will help them to decisively move toward the best outcome.

Remember, this is about finding a compatible match. You are not a fit for everyone, and everyone is not a fit for you. You are just here to help.

Regarding your area of expertise, you are the authority. There is no one better.

(These are things you should say to yourself as you show up to your appointment, whether in person on or video conference.)

Now you are ready for what I call: "OWN Pain SPA." It looks like this:

> Okay to say "no"
> Want – what do you want? Goals?
> Now – where are you now?
> **Pain**
> Story
> Plan
> Ask for commitment

O – Okay to Say "No"

The goal of the beginning of this conversation is to disarm your prospects' fight or flight mechanism by letting them know that they are in control.

You will do this by letting them know that it is okay to say "no" to you.

Other than removing the adversarial charge in the environment, purposefully letting them know that "no" is an okay answer has a few other benefits.

First, it shows that you are not desperate and that makes you more desirable.

Next, if you give someone the option to say "no," you are also giving them permission to say "yes."

Perhaps most importantly, it lets them know, nicely, that you will be asking for a decision at the end of your presentation.

Here is how it might sound:

> "Hey Suzi, before we begin, I want to let you know that this meeting is about you. I

really just want to understand where you are at and what you want to get accomplished, so I will be asking you several questions. If it makes sense, then I will share solutions that I might be able to provide. If I do, I just want to let you know, my solution is not a fit for everybody. If you look at it and it's not a good fit, that's okay, no big deal. Fair enough?"

W – Want

You really want to know what they are trying to get accomplished. Questions are the best calibrator and should be the focal point of the conversation. Be curious.

Here are several questions that would be appropriate (this list is only scratching the surface) to ask:

- What do you want?
- Where are you going?
- What are you trying to accomplish?
- What are your goals?
- Why is this important?
- What have you tried?

You can put any fact-finding questions you can think of here. Be sure to be interactive.

Do not read through your questions like a list or you will come off as interrogating.

N – Now

This is vital information you need to dig out:

- Where are you at now?
- How far is that from what you want?
- What is your reality?

Pain

This is perhaps the most difficult part of this process for nice people like you and me. We have to magnify their pain, so that we can prescribe a remedy.

If there is no pain, there is no sale. Just like a good doctor does not take patients at their word. Hardly! The doctor pokes and prods, always asking, "Does this hurt?" The purpose is to find you a remedy.

Be concerned for your prospect's problems as you do your examination.

Furthermore, you need to *sound* concerned. If someone told you they were having massive migraines, you would have empathy and your voice would show it.

Do the same thing here.

If you find them not sharing, holding their cards close to the vest, then you may want to start with something like:

> "Some of the problems that other companies like you are experiencing is _____. How are you dealing with that?"

Here are some examples of what to ask as you poke and prod to see their Pain:

- What are your obstacles?
- What happens if you continue as you are right now?
- How frustrating would that be?
- How does that feel?
- What is that costing you?
- What if nothing changes?
- What happens if you don't get there?
- Why is that so unacceptable to you?

S – Story

You will need to be ready with champion stories here. The goal is to make your prospects feel safe. They need to know you have been over this path a thousand times, and that you are more than capable of bringing them safely to their desired destination.

The key ingredients for a good story are a name, company name, time, place, pain, and outcome. It might go something like this:

> "You remind me of Bill Smith over at ABC Company, in Kearney, Nebraska. A year ago, before we started working together, he said their retention rates for new sales development reps was below 10%. He felt that was because they didn't have enough quality leads to call, which led to low success rates and burnout. He told me he could feel years of his life slipping away every time he tried to provide a new lead source. We implemented a new leads system called WEAPON X, and in less than a year, they were retaining more than 60% of the new salespeople they hired. I talked to him last week and he

says he is smiling. He calls us his 'Easy Button.' If I could show you how we did that for Bill, would that be a solution you could get excited about?"

P – Plan

This is the part your company has trained you on, except it's shorter. You present a couple of solutions they might go with. Be high level and give the schedule of what would happen and when. You are showing them your Plan.

The rule here is: be short and straight to the point. Most people can do this in 5-7 minutes. This should be the shortest part of your presentation.

Here is how it might sound and what it might include:

- "It sounds like the things you are trying to solve are A, B, and C. Is that right?"
- "And, if I'm understanding you, then what you think is most important is X, Y, and Z, did I hear you right?"
- "Can I share with you how we would go about that?"

- "This is how we would get you there."

Briefly describe your process on how you help clients get to the place that they described to you. For example:

> "With your company, I see a solution that would be similar to Sue Smith's. First, we analyze the type of leads you need. Next, we search our super powerful database to find out where those leads are. We then send connections to them via video, handwritten letters, and email. The end result is that your people have appointments created for them on their calendars."

A – Ask for commitment

Never *ever* give a solution without giving the price. Never *ever* give a price without asking for a commitment.

At the end of the presentation, there is nothing left to do except ask for the commitment. You have done your job. You have earned the right to ask for the sale. And you owe it to the person across from you to bring them to a conclusion.

Be the expert guide. Bring them across the finish line!

Now you are ready for commitment!

SELLING C#5: COMMITMENT

When I first started in sales, this was the most difficult part for me. Back then, I called it "closing." I knew this was the place where I found out if someone really liked me or not, and I was so afraid that they wouldn't.

The truth is, I probably wasn't so sure that I was providing the best solution. This unsure feeling could be so intense that it sometimes got in the way of me listening to my prospects.

The great news is in this process, gaining commitment is the easy part. Read that last sentence again.

Before we get into how to do it, I want to give you one nugget for your mindset. It is your job to bring people to a decision.

If we only educate and inform others, then we leave them in the valley of decision, which consumes so much emotion, energy, and time.

When you walk into a presentation, you must be convinced that it is your duty to serve people by helping them to come to a conclusion. Whether the conclusion is "yes" or "no" doesn't matter. Your goal is to help bring clarity to their direction. A "maybe" just won't do.

Here's the good news:

> You've been gaining commitments all along this process.

I want you to think about your interaction with your prospect like a road with stoplights. There's you in the driver's seat and the prospect in the passenger seat. You're not sure where they want to go, but every time you get to another stoplight, you ask them if they wish to keep going. "Yes," they confirm, and you drive on to the next stoplight.

At each light, you stop and ask again, do you want to keep going? You drive on to the next stoplight. And this continues until you get through all the stoplights and they are still in the car with you.

Ultimately, you can conclude that they want to go to the same place that you want to go.

If you've done your job at this point, you have asked them many questions and you've already been through all the stoplights. The final stoplight is the easiest. I call it the "Nice Guy Close."

The goal of the Nice Guy Close is to bring your prospect to a decision while maintaining the position of a guide, rather than taking on the role of the adversary.

Many deals die because the salesperson built a relationship and didn't know how to ask for the business in a manner that didn't feel like a mixed martial arts prize fight.

Remember your true motivation is an act of love, not war. Don't make it weird! Other than a confident servant's mindset, the most important part about the Nice Guy Close is before you ever get here, you must have in your mind the top solutions.

How to "Close" Like a Nice Guy

Before you reach this point, you must know your best-case outcome solutions. Let's call them Option A, Option B, and Option C.

You have them figured out, and you will simply ask the following:

> "It sounds like you're really experiencing X (pain) or Y (want). We should work together. Most people who are here either do Option A or Option B or Option C. Which of these makes the most sense to you?"

They can only say "yes" or "no" at this point. If they say "yes," then great. If they say "no," you simply ask, "Then what makes sense to you?"

That's it. Nothing fancy. No pressure, just a straight up ask.

Try it, and when they say "yes," be careful not to act surprised!

I credit the clarity of this method to my friend, James Muir, author of *The Perfect Close*. I encourage you to get his book and workbook now!

(Note: If you often find yourself entering into negotiation after this, I highly recommend picking up another resource, *Never Split the Difference* by Christopher Voss.)

That's it, right? Is this the end of the process?

No. Now comes the best part. If you are a genius practitioner of the sales process as described so far, you are a cut above the majority, but if you stop now, you are still missing the good stuff.

There is a promised land for the ones who have chosen sales as a path of virtue. A land flowing with milk and honey that most never dreamed possible. A place where hustle and 60-hour work weeks are just faint echoes of a bad dream.

This is the place we began at in the beginning, with you doing business with only the best people – you love them, and they love you.

These people actually refer you out all the time. They act like extensions of you, a volunteer sales force. Super fans, as it were.

I call them "champions." And you should know that the road to champions goes through consistency.

SELLING C#6: CONSISTENCY

The greatest sales method in the world is a promise fulfilled. This is your first commitment when someone says "yes" to you. It is your job to make sure that the promise is fulfilled.

It's easy to fall in love with someone who does what they said they would do. When you keep your promises, then you feel like you can take on the world.

However, your job is not finished here.

I remember hearing the story of a man who married a woman and never told her "I love you" after the day of their wedding. She complained, and he replied, "I told you I loved you once at the altar, and that ought to be enough for you forever."

I don't know if this story is true, but if it is, I can guarantee you this person probably did not have a happy marriage.

Here is a principle to consider:

> If you do what people expect you to do, they will trust you. If you do what they don't expect you to do, they will love you.

A client and lifelong friend, Timmy Ostrom, has built a multiple 9-figure business out of creating multiple unexpected moments for his clients and referral partners. He calls the program, "Share the Love."

There's a wonderful book written by Chip and Dan Heath called *The Power of Moments*. And one of the things they talk about is creating a client journey map. I've done this for my own business and have helped many clients do the same thing.

To sum it up, it goes something like this:

> Every client journey has a beginning and an end goal. In between the beginning and the goal, there should be mile markers along the way. Your job is to create an experience in which you celebrate milestone victories.

If you do this, you will make your clients feel awesome because you are reminding them of their success. You will also be reminding them of your participation in that success, and the journey ahead.

And guess what often happens next? (Mmm … do you smell a referral baking in the oven?)

It's not a bad idea to ask for referrals at every milestone where goodwill seems to be oozing in your direction. It is smart to acknowledge the milestones with a gift or a token of some sort.

I joined Weight Watchers and lost some weight, which was my goal, but I was pleasantly surprised to receive stickers, medals, and surprise envelopes as I completed different parts of my journey with them. Smart marketing!

Daniel, one of my clients who sold leads packages to insurance companies deployed these methods in a way that brought back crazy results. Even though his sales were very transactional (people would buy a package and he would never talk to them again), he still created a journey of shared experience and milestones.

We worked together to create a client journey where Daniel inserted himself into different parts of his client's journey and their interaction with the service he sold them. He offered different celebrations and trainings to his clients, and required them to be there, as though it was a part of his offering.

Somewhere in that process, we built in a space for him to ask for referrals. In doing so, Daniel, who was already the top sales guy in his company, multiplied his sales 5x over! He also accomplished the lowest churn rates in the company because his clients were better equipped to get the absolute most out of his service.

Consistency is important. You're building a sales machine, a furnace, that starts a chain reaction that never ends.

Selling is an act of love, not of war.

From this platform, you have earned the right to ask. Some people (your super clients, your super fans) will be invited into the circle, which is reserved for those of highest honor.

This is the place of champions.

SELLING C#7: CHAMPIONS

Champions are super clients. They are super fans. They are the ones you have served and delivered your promises for. They are the ones you want to duplicate, to multiply. And they are the people you want to build your business on.

The magical thing is, they multiply!

If you've been doing your job for more than a year, you probably already have champions. These are your clients who love you and you love them back. You are a great fit.

I have found it to be true that almost everyone knows one other person exactly like themselves or close to it. Yet most salespeople do an extremely poor job of asking for referrals.

Imagine that! If you could take your top client and double that person, double that business almost instantly, you would be insane to refuse such an opportunity … but we do it all the time!

Part of the reason we don't ask for referrals is because:

- we don't recognize champions
- we don't understand their value
- we don't know how to engage them
- we forgot how much they love us
- we forgot how much they want to help us

If you follow the steps listed in Selling C#6: Consistency, then asking for help and engagement from your champions is easy as pie.

Remember at the very beginning of the sales process we said that not everyone is a fit for you and you're not a fit for everyone? This, my friend, is why it is so important for you to recognize your champions.

Champions are the ones you should be building your business around and through. When people are benefiting greatly from your services or from your products, they are happy to share it with others.

They would be happy to send you referrals … if they only knew how to do so!

Before I tell you what to do with your champions, let me remind you that champions are your super fans, the ones who love you. They want to see you win.

Now, the most important thing when communicating with people:

> Make sure that the communication is calibrated with the relationship.

Do you still tell your mother or spouse what you do professionally? Of course not. That would be weird. They already know.

So, when interacting with your champions, you can skip the sales talk. Instead, you are going to be focusing on staying in their "top of mind" awareness, showing love, and engaging them in different ways.

Think of it this way ... if you want a happy marriage, you find ways to constantly communicate love to your spouse. If you forget, that's when things get bad.

But what happens when you say "I love you" to someone? Usually, as if by reflex, they repeat back, right?

The same thing happens with your champions. Your goal is to stay on their radar by saying, "I love you." By doing this one thing, you will receive countless referrals!

Why? Because you are top of mind. Because they remember you.

Don't just remember this. You might want to get it tattooed on your bicep:

> If you do what is *expected*, people will *trust* you. If you do the *unexpected*, they will *love* you.

How to Engage with Your Champions

I will give you a few ideas, but really, you should be the genius of love here. The playbook comes from you!

You want to come up with a few options that work for you. I have a few rules with this, just like with any habit. After all, you do want this to become habit!

> Rule 1: It must excite you.

Rule 2: It must be simple.

Rule 3: You must be able to dedicate a sanctioned, non-negotiable time to it.

So, as you look at the following list, select or create your top five ideas and ask yourself those questions: Does this excite me? Is it simple? Can I dedicate time for this?

Consider these options as you engage with your champions:

- call them to tell them you were thinking of them
- ask how you can serve them more
- text messages
- GIF texts
- text a video
- send a handwritten letter
- buy a wax seal for the handwritten letter (they are so cool, and only $20 on Amazon)
- sing happy birthday to them
- send cards for random holidays (Groundhog Day, National Ice Cream Day, etc.)

- send gift cards to them unexpectedly
- send a gift through Amazon
- buy something silly from a Dollar Store and send it with a note
- remember their anniversary, kids' names, favorite candy, etc., and send them these items unexpectedly
- send them thank you letters from *your children*
- send them a book that you love
- get a gift for them to give to their spouse or children or staff so they look like the hero

Collect Champion Stories

Every year, my family of ten has a tradition of Secret Santa shopping for one another. Gifts cannot exceed $20. The gifts are always interesting, and are a bit revealing about how much we truly know one another.

One year, my son Ephee drew my name, and after much deliberation, bought me a pack of thick tube socks. You know, the kind that skaters wear. Nice socks, but they were not really a match for me.

When explaining his decision, Ephee said, "I didn't know what you would want."

That's when I realized I had never told him!

Even if your clients love you, if you don't tell them what you want, they won't know what to do for you either.

This is what you want from your champions:

- success stories
- video testimonials
- referrals

A champion success story is a story of someone having success by engaging your product or service. You want these because in any scenario, the last person someone will believe is the biased opinion of a salesperson. However, we all believe stories.

Remember this:

> The most important sales tool you can possibly have is a steady supply of success stories.

Here are the reasons you want to obtain these as soon as humanly possible:

1. memorize them to build your belief in your own product/service
2. craft your own sales script
3. use on your website
4. use to overcome objections

You can do this a variety of ways, but do not leave it up to them to do or figure out. They are too busy.

Always remember:

> If you don't make it easy, don't expect to get the feedback you wanted.

Email Request

Here is an email template that I use. Customize it to your use.

> "Hey, my friend, I was hoping you could do me a favor. Could you provide your honest feedback on the impact of us working together? In an effort to make this easier on you, I took the liberty of

highlighting some of the story. Feel free to use this, alter it, or create something entirely new …

> I worked with Donnie as a producer and a recruiter. I have forked out multiple 6-figures on coaching, and seminars, so I am a junkie for self-improvement. My experience with Donnie and Purpose Driven Executive puts him at the top of the group. I was able to take action that was custom fit for ME. It's easy to act when the plan is designed with your skillset and desires in mind. That's what I did. No more sitting in front of a mirror for two hours to pump myself with positive self-talk. Now I LOVE what I do and who I do it for. I owe a part of that to Donnie!
> – Jim

Thank you!"

Video Testimonials Request

These are champion stories, but with a personal touch. A video testimonial is your client sharing for 30-90 seconds about how you delivered them to the promised land.

These are *extremely* powerful when it comes to someone deciding to spend time with you or to buy from you. Remember, in a sales conversation, and as far as a future prospect is concerned, if you say it, it might be false, but if someone else says it, it must be true.

The best way to get a video testimonial is after someone sends you a reply to the email above is to simply reply with:

> "Thank you so much! Hey, would you mind if I captured a quick and easy video of you saying the same thing? We can do it via Zoom, or you can just record it from your phone and send it to me."

Put these testimonials on your website or in your emails.

If someone is interested in my coaching services, I send them a link such as this one:

https://www.thesalesclassroom.com/testimonials

Use Your Success Stories

Once you have success stories, you should share them with your other clients. You might say, "Did you know we did this great thing for this company? Watch how this company solved this pain!"

This will help your champions to keep you top of mind, and more importantly, make the mental connections to their friends in business. Give them something to share, so they can say, "This guy or this company is great" as they refer business your way.

Always Ask for Connections

If you present your product or service without asking for the business, you are failing.

Likewise, if you are doing all these things and not asking for connections, then you are failing. Some people call these "referrals."

Asking for connections is the natural byproduct of being a good guy. You win. And whether you deserve it or not is irrelevant.

It's like this: When you plant and care for tomato plants, you get to pick tasty tomatoes.

On your journey, you must not be addicted to the idea of being the hero who fights for everything he has or being the one who outlasts everyone or the one who outworks everyone. I believe this is a mythology that is destroying families and lives of too many entrepreneurs and sales professionals. It requires you to give everything at work and have nothing left for home.

The Love Prospecting process is not about you being strong. Rather, it's about you being creative and being open to help from others.

A long time ago, Luke Skywalker could not have saved the galaxy without help from Han Solo and Chewbacca.

Neither can you. You must be willing to be helped by others. It might not be equal to the amount of effort you have put into this thing. It is often more!

That's why I call this part of my sales training process "Love Prospecting." Love makes work easier, and you usually receive more than you invest. Change your mindset to operating out of love.

Here is how asking for a connection might sound:

> "Timmy, I was hoping you could help me out. I have increased my capacity and I was wondering who do you know, who is _____ (description of your ideal client)? I am not going to force anybody to do business. As a matter of fact, they may not end up being a fit, but who do you know that I should meet? Who should I be talking to?"

Get names and write them down.

> "Cool. Thanks. Again, I am not going to attack them and sell them, so don't worry about that. Do you have their number? What do you like most about them? Why do you think I should talk to them?"

If it's helpful, you could add:

> "I don't want them to think I'm an ax murderer or anything. Can you make the introduction?"

During all of this, do not:

- use the word "referral"
- ask who needs your services
- make it hard on them
- be scared

And in all of this, make sure that you do:

- ask several times a year
- remind (not attack)
- ask for connections
- remind them you aren't an ax murderer

- ask for inside information that only a friend would know

From Connection to Prospect

Just because a friend sets you up on a blind date does not mean you need to make wedding plans. Likewise, just because your client connects you with someone does not mean you need to do business together. Even if you do, then you both need to come to the conclusion together.

So, handle it like a first date. Begin the conversation with your shared experience, which is your champion who connected you.

From there, follow the Love Prospecting process all the way through.

Conclusion

I can assure you that this works. I have traveled the hemisphere with my family, and done so successfully, selling from anywhere!

Our finances increased, not decreased, as we went along our journey.

You can live the life you have imagined. It just takes a little bit of engineering and some grit to push through.

And since you can sell from anywhere, what's stopping you?

Final Word

I hope you see the possibilities from all that you have read. Selling is serving. It is an act of love. So then, allow me one more opportunity to serve you.

If you want more, you can watch and listen as I break the whole process down in 17 minutes.

If this message resonates, you will find options that allow you to interact further. You know the drill, scan the following QR code or view it in your phone camera:

Your talent is NOT limited to your zip code, and if you can sell anywhere, you can sell everywhere.

www.GoSellAnywhere.com